Department of language Sciences Ca' Foscari University, Venice

Paolo E. Balboni

THE EPISTEMOLOGICAL NATURE OF LANGUAGE TEACHING METHODOLOGY

Guerra Edizioni

Language Acquisition and Learning: Document 1
General editor: Paolo E. Balboni

A publication of "Laboratorio ITALS – Teaching Italian to Speakers of Other Languages" within the Department of Language Sciences, Ca' Foscari University, Venice.

Title: The Epistemological Nature of Language Teaching Methodology
Author: Paolo E. Balboni
English translation: David Newbold
Publication No. 1 in the series
Year of Publication: 2006
© Copyright 2006, Guerra Edizioni, Via A. Manna, 25
06132 Perugia

ISBN 88-7715-899-9

Table of contents

1. LTM and the challenge of complexity

All mythologies have their golden age, when things were clear and simple, which are in sharp contrast with the present age in which things have become complex and difficult to analyse and act upon. The aim of this introductory chapter is to provide an overview of the increasing complexity of society and the parallel road taken by our area of research.

It is not our intention to seek causal connections, even if without a global effort in teaching and learning languages globalization would not have come into being, and without the drive towards globalization, modern language teaching methodology would not have developed; we can identify its beginnings in the response to the dramatic globalization which followed the Second World War, namely the ASTP (see below).

What we are interested in is to see how society and LTM have changed profoundly since the appearance of a whole range of major variables which have made the system of links and relations between parts of a *système où tout se tient* ever more complex. But it is not just the number of inter-related variables which has changed, increasing the structural complexity of the system: the nature of individual variables has changed too. One example will make this clear: throughout nearly the whole of the twentieth century China was a simple element, governed simply (i.e., predictably) initially by the Emperor and, following the communist revolution, by the Party; but since the 1990's everything has changed: 'China' has become a concept the meaning of which is exceedingly complex, whether considered from the point of view of internal relations or in its relations with other actors on the world stage; in LTM, until the 1970's, we had the clear and simple notion that 'children have great cerebral plasticity during the first years of their lives', but over the past two decades the useful metaphor of *plasticity* has had to be replaced following a series of neurolinguistic studies which describe the process of language acquisition with data which start with the first seconds of life and map the whole process in an extremely complex manner.

So to the 'horizontal' complexity, which is a result of the increase in nodes in the networks of society and consequently of LTM, we have to add the 'vertical' complexity which makes every node complex internally.

In this chapter we will start from the above reflections and attempt to establish a basis for analyzing the epistemological complexity of a LTM whose aim is to meet the needs of the global society - a society which can exist only if languages are taught and learnt effectively, and in which LTM is an important part of the progression from a world stage which had only a few main actors (the great 19th century empires and the superpowers of the Cold War period) to a mosaic which is changing continuously, rapidly, and unpredictably.

1.1 From simplicity to complexity in LTM: the 20th century

In the history of LT there is a sort of 'Golden Age', when things were clear and simple: teaching the mother tongue meant teaching the standard language, based on literary models and strictly controlled by grammar rules; teaching classical languages meant to teach their grammar and lexis in order to approach literary works; teaching foreign languages was not really different from teaching Latin.
With the beginning of the 20th century some of these certainties collapsed:

The trend, then, in language sciences during the initial and central part of the century is one which goes from simplicity to complexity. (For further reading see Balboni 2002).

1.2 Social complexity and the request for a new LTM

a. Saussure divided *langue*, which had been the object of LTM so far, from *parole*, opening the way to sociolinguistics half a century later. The first question this raised was: Should a teacher (and by 'teacher' we mean curriculum designers, textbook writers, evaluators, etc.) present students with *langue* or *parole*? Early in the 20th century Palmer, Jespersen and Sweet tried to face this new complexity and opened the way to a LTM revolution which was to explode half a century later, during World War II, with the US Army Specialized Training Program and its focus on *parole* and on the relation between language and culture;

Cassirer, Bühler and Jakobson studied language as function rather that form, opening the way to Austin, Searle and Halliday and, eventually, to the functional method in language teaching, to the
b.   threshold levels, and to the Common European Framework which came at the end of the 20th century;
Chomsky, although maintaining that his studies are of no use to LTM, destroyed other principles of the golden age: acquisition no longer depended on Bloomfield and Skinner's mechanical repetition
c.   and pattern drills, because the *Language Acquisition Device* works by observing the input it receives, making hypotheses, and testing them; *knowing* a language differs from *cognizing* it, i.e. knowing about it; language is generated by *competence* so that the aim of LT is creating competence, working on processes rather than mere products, i.e. *performance*. Krashen was to rely heavily on Chomsky's principles for his universally known *Second Language Acquisition Theory*.

In a society composed of different states, international organisations, and multinational companies, we find a trend from simplicity towards complexity, which parallels the trend in LTM. In the society which emerged during the second part of the century the need to study languages became greater than ever before.
During the first part of the century the imposition of national languages had led to the disappearance of local languages and dialects, creating the illusion of a simplification of the linguistic context. Today these languages have themselves been reduced to the status of local languages in the context of globalisation. The solution of using a lingua franca which appeared in the last decades of the 20th century - English, often reduced to little more than a pidgin - also turned out to be illusory. Instead of simplifying, it brought into contact the enormous, complex diversity of the world and made the problems of intercultural communication more obvious (Balboni 1999).
During the 1970s and 1980s English language teaching grew massively. This phenomenon stemmed from a primitive idea of communication, namely, that an instrument for global communication, identified as the *threshold level*, would break down barriers and create a bridge between speakers of different language blocks: for example, the eleven

language communities of the European Community would finally be able to speak to each other, and they would also be able to speak to the Arab world, to China, and to Latin America. This may have been true at a high level, for academics, politicians, managers and tourist operators, but in reality for millions of people English became the tool which gave rise to new transnational sub-communities who shared the same interests in music, sports, or politics, or who had the same economic background. These sub-communities existed in real space opened up by Maastrict and Schengen, but also, and especially, in the virtual space created by the mass media for specific audiences, such as VideoMusic, Eurosport and Eurotika. At the same time the World Wide Web was breaking up into numerous fragments, each a self contained universe, with its own clientele - pedophiles, linguists, music lovers, and adepts of fringe religions, such as druids and technobuddhists, to name but a few.

The 1990's were a crucial moment in this transition towards complexity. In the United States the unifying motti *E pluribus unum* came under threat from the wave of Hispanic and Asian immigrants who had no wish to disappear in the melting pot. The EU found a different political response, of considerable strategic importance, to the problem of reshuffling old communities and forming new ones, when it affirmed that 'linguistic and cultural difference is a founding value of the Union' and adopted, in article 126 of the treaty of Maastricht, the principle by which linguistic pluralism is recognized as a valuable resource which should be preserved: every citizen has the duty to study, not only his or her mother tongue, but also two other languages of the Eu - English as a lingua franca, and another language chosen as much for pleasure as for necessity.

But the 21st century has brought with it yet another complexity - a tide of poor immigrants on both sides of the Atlantic, while rich immigrants (e.g., the technicians of Euro-American multinationals) set off to India, China and Brasil. All these immigrants - whether poor or rich, slaves or technocrats - take their languages with them, as well as their own restaurants and films, making the society in which they arrive more complex, but whose language they still need to learn, adding complexity to their own minds and personal histories...

1.3 Synthesis

In simple societies, language teaching was simple: it focussed on the standard variety of the mother tongue, and on presenting texts in Latin and a foreign language, usually French.
Today the complexity of society had led to a more complex approach to language teaching:

- *the notion of 'knowing a language' has been clearly articulated*, for example in the various levels of the Common European Framework and the American Standards;
- *reasons for learning have been clearly articulated*: English is based on needs, while other languages have to offer an intrinsic interest to be motivating;
- *the profile of the student has changed*; during the Golden Age languages were studied by adolescents; today learning begins at Primary School and continues beyond school in programmes of lifelong learning; in the past a student was simply a 'student', but today we take into consideration a variety of different needs and aims, different cognitive styles, and different learning strategies;
- as a result, *the typology of texts to be used has changed* - no longer just literary texts to be read, but oral texts, dialogues, e-mails and so on; and so have t*he typologies of teaching techniques, technologies, teachers, courses* and *assessment*.

The progressive complexity of society and of LTM are inter-dependent; we know that globalisation and social complexity cannot exist without linguistic interchange, and that they need a new kind of language teaching. But this is not just a matter of approach, method, techniques and technologies used. Rather, the problem needs to be approached on the epistemological level:

a. What sort of knowledge is needed to be able to teach a language? Theoretical, applicative, or implicative? Syncretic or analytic? Linear or hypertextual?
b. What are the sources of knowledge in LTM?
c. How can LTM knowledge be translated into LTM skills?

d. How can this knowledge be evaluated? By assessing 'effectiveness' (but how can we define 'effective' in LT?) or by taking into account principles of internal coherence and successive processes of falsification and validation of this knowledge itself?

In this first issue of a series of 'Documents', we will attempt to answer these questions; in the Documents which follow we shall examine the applications of this epistemological approach in a variety of different sectors and environments.

2. Native, Foreign, Second, Ethnic, Classical, Artificial Languages

LTM is the science that studies the processes of language – any language – teaching (and, of course, acquisition: the latter being implied by our use of the term 'teaching'). The word 'language' in the statement above can be seen to refer to at least six different things, and as a result there are at least six different LTMs.

2.1 Mother tongue

'Mother tongue' seems to be an intuitively clear notion, but in fact it is very complex.
Neurobiology offers a clear definition: tests carried out on the heart beat of new born infants, just 60 seconds after birth, and therefore not influenced in any way by the social environment, have shown that, after the stress of birth, the infant calms down on hearing the mother tongue; a baby whose mother is a Russian living in France recognizes the sounds and rhythms of Russian, not those of French. But this definition, which is extremely relevant for neurolinguistics, is not appropriate in a context of LTM, where by 'mother tongue' we mean the language of the home environment, in which the child grows, thinks (but bilingual children think in more than one language), cries out in pain, or makes rapid mental calculations when playing cards.
Teaching the mother tongue has a precise function: to systemize and improve the quality of a language which, when the speaker starts his or her formal education, has already been acquired.
Mother tongue teaching thus shares with other LTMs the notions of approach, method and technique (see point 3), a cross-curricular epistemology (see points 4-6), a repertoire of teaching techniques, and organisational models such as syllabus, module, teaching unit, lesson, etc., but it applies these towards a different aim - not towards the acquisition of a new language, but to the improvement of one which has already been acquired.
As the LTM context changes, the source of complexity changes: a reading test which uses the same passage and the same techniques differs

according to whether it is used for the mother tongue or a foreign language. The child's mind is subjected to stress since he or she has to realize that the same task (for example: to read a text and answer multiple choice questions based on it) requires cognitive and linguistic strategies which differ according to whether the text is in the mother tongue or another language; but he or she, at least until late adolescence, is unable to analyse his or her own strategies, or cognitive and linguistic processes, and so is unaware of the complexity of the situation.

2.2 Foreign language and second language

These terms are a frequent cause of confusion, not only among teachers, but also at institutional level (for example *FLE, français langue étrangère* is used in both contexts) and by academics: the most notorious case is to be found in Krashen's *Second Language Acquisition Theory*, which the author, as well as other writers, sometimes ascribes to foreign language, not just second language, learning contexts. In addition, linguists as well as psychologists, often use 'L2' to refer to any language learnt after the mother tongue, L1.

For the purposes of LTM these definitions seem useful:

	Foreign language	*Second language*
Presence in the environment	A foreign language is not present in the environment in which it is studied, as is the case with, for example, English in Algeria.	A second language is present in the environment, for example, English studied by an Algerian in Britain; this is the case with the host language for immigrants. or in bilingual areas such as Catalonia or South Tyrol.
Selection and grading of input	The teacher controls this; he or she chooses the materials, knows what has already been presented and what has been acquired. Only for English is there further input (songs and films) which circulates in the mass media and is beyond the teacher's control.	The pupil is immersed in the second language, which means that the teacher has no control of the input, nor of what and how much the pupils has acquired spontaneously (and sometimes with errors) in daily life.

The role of the teacher	The teacher provides the principal model for the spoken language, even when other models (such as CDs and video) are available.	The teacher is not the model for the spoken language; pupils frequently claim that the teacher's language is too 'correct', i.e. inappropriate or too formal for the contexts in which they find themselves outside school, lacking informal registers (colloquial and vulgar) that they need in everyday life.
Teaching activities	In many cases the techniques used are based on false premises: one only has to think of a role play in which two people who share the same mother tongue, and who live near each other, and who have spent years together both at school and elsewhere, are made to speak together in a foreign language to say things which *simulate* reality. This simulation is even more marked in the relation between teacher and pupil, since the teacher almost invariably knows the answers to the questions she asks.	In some cases there can be simulation, as with foreign language teaching, but in most cases the teacher is able to ask genuine questions, which refer to real life situations in the country in which the second language is spoken. The use of role play in a L2 may be authentic communication since the L2 is often the only language shared by students.
Syllabus and course design	The teacher and teaching materials follow a syllabus, which is often set out in the course book; this syllabus is followed scrupulously.	The teacher needs to refer to a syllabus, but cannot follow it scrupulously since the L2 pupil brings to the classroom questions which require answer; if the teacher wants to finish teaching the comparative, but the student says he doesn't understand how to use the gerund, the teacher will have to give a lesson on verbs and not adjectives.

Testing and assessment	The teacher is aware of what he or she has taught, knows what minimum requirements have been set, knows what has been achieved (or should have been achieved) in previous lessons, and thus knows what to assess, and how to evaluate acquisition.	The teacher has faced a number of aspects of the L2 together with the student, but many others have been acquired spontaneously; the teacher cannot include these in a collective test, since each student has followed a different learning path. As a result, formal tests tend to be replaced by continual error analysis and feedback.
Use of technology	It is essential in FL teaching to complement the model offered by the teacher, to present authentic materials, different voices, culture, and to make real communication possible through the use of e-mail, web cams, etc.	It is not essential.

As can be seen, even if we refer to the same language (English in Algiers and English in London), the two contexts, L1 and L2, require different texts, different technologies, and different methodologies to meet the specific needs of the contexts[1].

2.3 Ethnic language

By 'ethnic language' we mean a specific form of second language, spoken in the original community of a person who has not acquired it as a

---

[1] The philosophy of *foreign* language teaching developed by the Venice group is apparent in a range of publications which are the result of nearly forty years of research: Freddi 1970, 1979 and 1994, Balboni 1991, 1994 and 2002; in *second* language teaching, which became relevant to the Italian context only towards the end of the 1990's, there are publications by Balboni (2000), Luise (2003, 2006), and Santipolo (2005), Caon (2005) as well as dozens of articles in volumes dedicated to teacher education, such as Dolci and Celentin (2003). Serragiotto (2004) and Pavan (2005).

mother tongue but who nonetheless hears it spoken in the family environment (for example, the children of parents of different nationalities) or within an immigrant community; for example, the children and grandchildren of Italian immigrants in Germany often grow up as German speakers but may hear Italian spoken at home and by friends of parents or on dedicated radio or TV programmes.

In America a further distinction is made between *family language*, spoken by immigrant families living in areas in which there are no other immigrants from the same origins (Francescato speaks of 'isolated bilinguals'), and *community language*, where an ethnic community exists, and so the ethnic language is used outside as well as inside the home. Parents, and students too, after adolescence, often want to go back to their family roots, and thus try to recover the *ethnic* language, but compared with a *second* language context there are a number of problems:

a. it is true that the ethnic language is spoken in the environment in which the person lives, and so he or she may have been able to acquire it spontaneously, at least in part; but it is also true that a language acquired only by listening to parents and their friends is hardly ever the standard language in the country from which they originate, since immigrants usually come from social classes with a less than complete knowledge of the standard variety. Furthermore, the parents and their friends will have left their home country twenty or thirty years previously, and provide an obsolete model of the language. Thus, when the student decides to perfect his knowledge of this language that he has learnt spontaneously, by enrolling in a course, he discovers to his great dismay that what he has been listening to is not Spanish but Andalucian, not Italian but Neapolitan, not Romanian but Moldavian, and that the teacher considers what he has picked up spontaneously as more of a hindrance than a help; in short, he discovers that what he knows (and, in an ethnic context, what he *is*) is wrong...

b. since the ethnic environment makes use of non-standard forms which are not completely acceptable, the teaching of the ethnic language inevitably tends towards the norm of foreign language teaching. This rationale may be justified, but it is likely to demotivate the student if he becomes aware of it: he is studying Spanish, Italian or Romanian because he already knows it in part, but if this knowledge is useless, why bother to continue with the language?

2.4 Lingua franca

Two thousand years ago it was Latin, today it is English: a lingua franca is a language which is normally used in a fairly simplified form (but without acquiring the characteristics of a *pidgin*) to facilitate international communication.
The growth of English as a lingua franca has completely changed the nature of the way in which the language is taught, even if officially we still speak of 'English as a foreign language'. When English is taught as a lingua franca:

a. a preoccupation with British or American culture disappears; in fact, teaching materials often choose to ignore cultural features such as the use of pork or alcohol, or the way people behave in society, since it is assumed that they will not be used by students in New York or Edinburgh. The student of a lingua franca wants the language, not the culture; the terrorists who brought down the Twin Towers in New York wanted to learn the language perfectly to be able to destroy the culture;

b. the aim is not to be able to speak with a pronunciation resembling that of a native speaker, but to be understood by everybody. The need to know English as a lingua franca is obliging British, Americans, and Australians to learn this international variety of the language, and to reduce the range of their own registers and personal preferences; they have to learn to keep to a *bad English* which everyone, except for themselves, seems able to understand and to speak;

c. the lexis is reduced, with synonyms being the first words to be lost; the achievement of the aim, successful communi-cation, is far more important than formal accuracy, especially in 'useless' markers such as the third person *s*, the sequence of tenses, or the past tense of certain irregular verbs.

When people of different cultural backgrounds attempt to communicate using English as a lingua franca the main problems of intercultural communication come to the fore, and the complexity of the teaching reaches its highest levels; if, for example, we are teaching English to managers of a multinational who are going to use the language primarily in meetings and project presentations, then they need to be taught what Hofstede calls *softwares of the mind*: a sense of time (and hence, punctuality, the rules of turn taking and when to keep silent, etc.), hierarchy, status, verbal forms of respect (in formal registers), and non-verbal forms (bowing, avoiding eye contact, etc.); we have to allow ample space in the syllabus for a range of non verbal forms of communication (kinesic, proxemic, and so on) because non-verbal communication (in the form of a gesture, for example) will always be more significant than the language with which it is accompanied[2].

2.5 Classical language

Koranic Arabic and Mandarin Chinese are both 'classical' languages in the sense that nobody speaks them as their mother tongue, but their prestige comes from texts and traditions which are still alive, and they are often used as a lingua franca across the Arabic-speaking or Chinese-speaking world; Greek and Latin are 'classical languages' in the sense that they are no longer used for communicative purposes (except in the Roman Catholic Church, where Latin still has an official role) but they are the language of those literary, philosophical and juridical texts on which Western civilisation is based.
'Dead language' to refer to Greek or Latin is a misnomer, since Homer, Catullus, Plato and Seneca still speak to us through their writings; but they can become dead languages for students if the methodology used makes use of an arid mix of grammar rules and word lists.
A number of approaches used in foreign language teaching have been applied to the teaching of Greek and Latin, but with notable differences:

---

2 On intercultural communication, and the illusion that this may be achieved using English as a lingua franca, see Balboni 1999 and Pavan 2006.

a. recreating the oral dimension may be justified for receptive purposes (such as listening to an extract from Homer) but not for production; only cardinals use Latin to speak, during a conclave;

b. *the functional/pragmatic dimension* may be justified, for example when producing a play, but is less significant than in the context of modern language teaching, where the communicative approach has become the keystone;

c. *the cultural dimension*, whether explicit in the text, or implicit in the lexis, is fundamental, and without parallel in other teaching contexts; if we continue to study Latin and Greek it is to have direct access to a cultural heritage which is part of our DNA

d. modern technology offers the possibility to recreate a physical and cultural environment (for example, through computer-generated reconstructions of Rome, Athens or Pompeii) which give indications about life styles (two recent films, *Troy* and *Alexander* are very accurate in this respect, and as such could be a useful teaching aid); but technology does not offer examples of language in use, unlike what happens in all the other situations described in this chapter

e. the aim in studying Greek or Latin is not to learn grammar, or to learn to read and understand a text, but to penetrate the culture from which we originate, as Euro-Americans; so the possibility of assessing acquired competence through performance (understanding a text by Cicero) is practically non-existent.

One problem facing teachers of classical languages is the fact that students start them after years of contact with English as a foreign language, or as a lingua franca, and perhaps with other languages too; so he or she starts with a pre-conceived idea about what it means to learn a language, and how to go about doing so, with the risk of being unpleasantly surprised to find that the procedures for Greek and Latin are very different, without really understanding why.

2.6 Artificial Language

The past century saw the creation of a number of artificial or 'international' languages, but only one of these - Esperanto - has survived. In contrast, fans of other worlds crowd the Internet to enrol in on-line courses in Klingan (the language of the aliens in Star Trek) or Hobbit-speak from Tolkien's *Lord of the Rings*.

Another growing dimension for artificial languages is sign languages, used to communicate with, and by, the deaf.

From a structural and lexical point of view artificial language are simple, linear, and logical, at least for an educated European. This simplicity creates the illusion that these languages are equally easy to teach. And in theory Esperanto could be an easy language to teach, but only on the condition that the student wants to learn it, and has a strong ideological motivation to do so (and the ideology which Esparantists promote does not make them popular with other LT methodologists, since they resemble French teachers calling for a ban on teaching barbarian languages such as English...). In other words, the student's motivation, and his or her knowledge of other European languages - classical or modern - play a more important role than they do in learning foreign, ethnic, or second languages. Only with classical languages is motivation as fundamental as it is with Esperanto.

2.7 Synthesis

In the Golden Age of LTM the grammar of the national language, of Latin and of French, was taught using the same terms ('pronoun', 'adverb', 'subject', 'predicate', 'case', etc.) with the aim of preparing the student to read the canonical texts of a shared culture. Perfecting the mother tongue had a high communicative aim, but learning French and Latin (and music, too, for that matter) had a further, non-linguistic, aim: it showed you belonged to a high social class. The analysis that we have made in this chapter would thus have been pointless a century ago.

Today we study languages to communicate, in the widest sense of the term; the situations in which languages are taught are extremely varied, as we have seen, and this complexity makes it necessary for curriculum planners, materials writers, and language teachers to make informed choices - which begin with a pondered choice of the first letter of the LTM acronym, 'language' – which is a complex choice as it can mean at least six different things.

3. Theory, Approach, Method and Technique

In this chapter we shall consider the complex nature of LTM in its function of identifying, categorizing and validating (or falsifying) the range of knowledge which allows us to teach languages and to be able to make an adequate response to the complexity of the contexts in which we carry out the teaching.

The traditional conflict (which we will return to in chapters 4 and 5) between theoretical sciences, whose aim is to know, and practical sciences, whose aim is to solve problems, has often led to LTM being seen as an 'applied' science; in other words, there was theoretical linguistics, and there was LTM which 'applied' that knowledge; the model was simple. In reality things are more complex, since there are at least four types of 'knowledge' involved in LTM:

The conceptual complexity can be clearly stated thus:

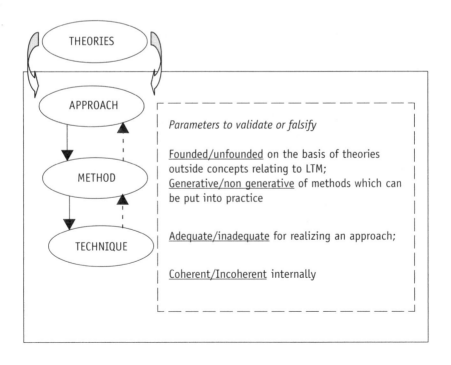

Some theoretical sciences (such as linguistics, neurology, psychology, and anthropology), as well as some practical sciences (such as pedagogy and methodology) have provided us with 'theories' of reference. As can be seen above, these lie *outside* the world of LTM, which makes use of them to obtain the information it needs to be able to fulfil its function - to hypothesise and create paths for language acquisition and linguistic education.

There are three levels of knowledge in LTM, and as a consequence, there are three levels of action: approach, method, and technique. We will try to show how the complexity of the knowledge provided by theoretical sciences generates these three levels of knowledge in LTM, and which parameters are used to evaluate an approach, a method, or a technique; the definition of these parameters (indicated in the table above) is fundamental since it is these parameters which make it possible to accept, or to reject, an approach, a method, or a teaching technique.

3.1 Approach

Those areas of knowledge relating to 'approach', and which come from linguistic and cultural sciences, from pyschology and from educational sciences (see chapter 4 for a detailed discussion), can help us to define

a. *a concept of language*: for decades, languages have been seen as instruments of communication, and being able to use the language effectively comes primarily from linguistic correctness and situational appropriacy;

b. *a concept of culture*, cultural contact and conflict, and differences between stereotype and sociotype;

c. *a model of the learner*, by attributing specific roles to the two hemispheres of the brain, and hence distinguishing cognitive styles which favour the big picture and intuition, or by contrast, analysis and rationality, and to different learning strategies and different types of motivation;

d. *the aim of language education*, as part of the wider educational process, and the *specific aims of language teaching*, which are listed in a syllabus.

An approach is thus a philosophy of language, of the student (and hence the teacher), and of the syllabus, as well as the context in which we define the scientific premises for 'methods' which can render an approach operative.

If we look at the history of LTM in the 20th century we can see that grammar-translation, the direct method, and the reading method (although traditionally called 'methods'), as well as the audio-lingual, structuralist, communicative and natural approaches, are all in fact 'approaches', in the sense that they are full-blown theories of language education[3]. The humanistic and the constructivist approaches, by contrast, although known as such, are in fact methodologies, in that they consist only of one component of the neuro-pyschological component of LTM (see 3.2).

An approach can be evaluated on

a. the scientific basis of the theories whose principles it uses;
b. its internal coherency, by applying the non-contradiction principle;
c. its capacity to generate methods; an approach which has a scientific basis, and internal coherency, but which has no practical applications, i.e. it does not generate methods, is of no use to LTM, which, by its epistemological nature, is 'to solve problems through knoweldge'.

3.2 Method (and methodology)

A 'method' is a combination of methodological principles which convert an approach into operational models, teaching materials, ways of using technologies, and relational models between teachers and students and between students.

The situational method and the notional/functional method are examples of 'methods' which come from the communicative 'approach'.

A method is not 'right' or 'wrong', or 'good' or 'bad', as one often hears in debates between traditionalists and innovators in LTM, but should be evaluated on

---

3 The Venice group has always worked within the context of a communicative approach: first in its realization of the situational method, in Freddi (1970 and 1979) and later with the functional method, in Freddi (1994) and Balboni (1991, 1994 and 2002) as well as in the previously mentioned materials for teacher education.

a. its ability to make the philosophy of the approach which it is based on operational;
b. its internal coherency;
c. its ability to select techniques which are coherent with the method from the range of teaching techniques available;
d. its ability to identify ways of using technology which are integrated with the other components of the method, and which respect the premises of the approach[4].

A clarification needs to be made to distinguish between two terms: *method*, which derives from an approach in the model *approach → method → technique*, as defined by Anthony; and *methodology*, which has two meanings:

a. it describes the complex of principles and actions which are brought to bear to achieve a teaching aim (in our case, the acquisition of a language); and in this sense it is part of the LTM acronym - and we shall continue to use the term, not without some misgivings, within our epistemological parameters;
b. it gives a particular colour when used to denote a method: *humanistic and affective methodology*, which underlines the role of the emotions and respect for the whole person (a feature of the Venice school since the 1990s), and which gives prominence to a *games based methodology* which makes use of techniques based on play as ends in themselves, a source of pleasure and interaction, and *a workshop methodology*[5]; there is also a *CLIL methodology*[6].

---

4 Roberto Dolci of the Venice group has been working in this field for many years. He is the author of a number of articles in volumes referred to *passim*, in particular Porcelli and Dolci 1999.
5 Games based methodology has been studied by the Venice group in Caon and Rutka (2003), and workshop methodology, which features in many of the teacher education volumes referred to above, is studied in depth in Caon (2005) and Caon and D'Annunzio (2006).
6 Two Venice researchers who have studied the problem are Coonan (2001) and Serragiotto (2004).

In short, we have to be careful to distinguish between 'method', used in a hierarchical epistemology to indicate the moment at which a philosophy of language teaching (or 'approach') is converted into a classroom operation (or 'technique'), and 'methodology' which indicates a specific characteristic of a way of teaching.

3.3 Technique

A technique is a teaching action used to achieve an objective; techniques are not usually universal, suitable for every kind of intelligence, and every learning strategy, and so they need to be chosen in such a way that they do not penalize one type of personality compared to another. In practice, there are two types of techniques:

a. *exercises*, which require the manipulation of language, and are aimed more at consolidation than use: they include pattern drills, transformation exercises, matching, and, in some cases, cloze and dictation;
b. *activities*, which are more creative, based on solving problems by using the target language; they include role plays, letter writing, reporting, and dictation when it is the first step in another activity, such as a role play.

Techniques are not 'good' or 'bad' or 'modern' or 'old fashioned', but are to be evaluated simply on

a. their ability to achieve the aims of the approach and the method: e.g., a translation is not a suitable means of achieving the aims of a communicative approach;
b. conceptual coherence with the method and approach which it belongs to: a dictation is not coherent with the premises of a communicative approach which puts the accent firmly on play, unless the dictation is transformed into a game (and is corrected by the student);
c. effectiveness and efficiency in achieving the teaching objective; within a communicative approach a cloze or a matching activity are effective, and also, given their ease of execution, and the wide range

of processes which they activate, efficient; a pattern drill much less
so, since there are fewer occasions on which it can be used.

In the Italian tradition of LTM, which has a large number of applied
linguists, there has been little reflection on techniques, as if the fact
that they come at the bottom of the epistemological model we are
discussing had made them irrelevant as an object of study. The Venice
group, by contrast, has always paid great attention to this level of the
epistemological model[7].

3.4 Synthesis

The three levels of articulation reveal the complex nature of knowledge
in LTM: on the one hand, we have to identify the boundaries between
what it includes (approach, method, technique), and what lies outside
(theories of reference), while within the context of action in LTM we
have to distinguish between three levels of knowledge:

a. theoretical-philosophical knowledge;
b. organisational knowledge;
c. operational knowledge.

In this case the complexity of LTM does not derive from the complexity
of society or an increase in theoretical research, but from its nature as
a practical science.
In other words, the simplicity of the Golden Age, which we will discuss
in the review of approaches in Chapter 6, was an illusion, due to a lack

---

7 The key text in Italy for teaching techniques was conceived in Venice (Balboni
1991), and has been reissued in various editions; the Venice group is also responsible
for numerous articles in volumes which we have cited *passim*, and a series for Guerra
Edizioni in which, after an in-depth theoretical reflection, teaching techniques relevant
to the specific problems raised are presented, for example a games-based LTM (Caon
and Rutka 2004), a workshop based LTM (Caon and D'Annunzio 2006), teaching Italian
to foreigners from a linguistic and comparative anthropological standpoint (Celentin
and Cognigni 2005, Della Puppa 2005, D'Annunzio 2006, with others to follow).

of reflection on the nature of LTM. This state of affairs was not the fault of Vietor, Jespersen, Berlitz, Palmer, Sweet, or the other great exponents of LTM, but was due to a lack of intellectual challenge; since LTM only had to meet the limited objectives of language teaching as it was conceived at the end of the nineteenth and the beginning of the twentieth centuries, it was not necessary to reflect too much. But if they had reflected, they too would have come up with a complex model, inasmuch as this complexity, as we have pointed out, is an intrinsic part of the nature of LTM.

4. From theory to practice, from application to implication

In this chapter we shall try to indicate the mechanisms by which theoretical knowledge is transferred to LTM from the outside, following Freddi (in Porcelli and Balboni 1991) who, perhaps more than anyone else, has examined the question. (See table in chapter 3)
To do so we need to reapply the Aristotelian distinction between theoretical sciences, practical sciences, and applied sciences.

4.1 Theoretical sciences, applied sciences, practical sciences

In epistemology there is a distinction between those sciences which

a. aim at knowledge and are called *theoretical*; for example, the aim of biology is knowledge of the nature of life; chemistry aims to decribe how atoms combine in molecules; linguistics aims to know the nature and function of language;
b. aim at solving problems and are called *practical* or *operational*; the aim of medicine is to resolve pathologies of human or animal biology; pharmacology seeks those molecules which can be used in medicine; LTM aims to respond to the need to learn languages and to be able to use them.

So we are dealing with two different worlds: one is cognitive, the other operative. Nonethless, while nobody has ever confused theoretical biology with operational medicine, or theoretical chemistry with pharmaceutics, throughout the second half of the 20th century there was the illusion that there could be a *simple* path from theoretical linguistics to the operational context of LTM: the *application*. Today, half of the research in LTM in Italy is still considered to be 'applied linguistics', and in many contexts LTM is still seen as a synonym for *applied linguistics, linguistique appliquée,* etc.
In reality, the theoretical sciences can only be applied to specific aspects: for example, linguistics can be applied to translation, to textual analysis (e.g. of scientific or professional texts), and so on, and become *applied linguistics,* while remaining within a theoretical context, and whose aim is knowledge.

But as soon as there is a problem to be solved, and not merely described, the theoretical science - pure, uncontaminated, defined within its own clear limits, and therefore 'simple' - is usually no longer sufficient, since the reality in which problems have to be resolved is complex. It is for this reason that the practical sciences, including LTM, tend to be interdisciplinary, based on more than one theoretical and applied sciences, and on other practical sciences, from which they derive implications which can help in solving the problem.

LTM is not an application of linguistics, because linguistics knows nothing (nor does it want to) of the processes of acquisition of knowledge, of the management of intra-class relations, of the problems of intercultural communication, of syllabus design, and so on.

4.2 The principles of application and implication

We stated above that LTM does not belong to the *applied* sciences but that it is interdisciplinary, and seeks to draw *implications* from sciences which, in the table in chapter 3, lie outside the specific context of LTM. There is no word play intended between *application* and *implication*, but a necessary choice to determine who it is who decides which sources of knowledge to draw from, and how to use them:

a. in a context of *LTM as applied linguistics* the subject is a linguist who applies his knowledge to LTM, and allocates only secondary importance to the second part of the LTM acronym - teaching methodology;

b. in a context of *LTM as an interdisciplinary science* the subject is the LT methodologist, who takes what he needs from various sciences to solve the problem, on the basis of the objectives which have been set, and the context.

In other words, *application* is a simple response to a complex problem, and is therefore insufficient. Many people believe it is *the* response, but this is an error. In recent years linguists have attempted to move in a more interdisciplinary direction, coming up with the notion of *educational linguistics*, but without changing the substance: the noun is still *linguistics*, the rest is an adjective which distinguishes this application' from other applications of linguistics.

4.3 Synthesis

LTM does not have the primary aim of knowing what it means to acquire a language, but the solution of the problem of how to make acquisition take place. So it is not a theoretical science, but a practical, operational one.

In the past it was believed that to teach languages it was sufficient to apply linguistic theory: *applied* linguistics, based on this principle, gave us the grammar-translation approach and is responsible for its failures; taxonomic linguistics and behaviourist psychology led to the structuralist approach, and precisely because of the mechanical nature of the application they are responsible for the failure of this approach too.

In contrast, the direct approach, the communicative approach, and the natural approach, have all come not from the theoretician who applies, but from someone on the spot who has to find a practical solution to a problem (how to teach a language as an instrument of communication) and who has been able to locate useful *implications* in the sciences of language, communication, culture, the person, and education.

Our conclusion is thus that *LTM is an operational and interdisciplinary science.*

5. The epistemological universe of LTM

Where does LTM find the knowledge it needs to be able to carry out its task?
Which sciences lie outside the context of the table in chapter 3?
From which sciences can LTM draw implications?
Because of the complexity of the problem it has to resolve, LTM derives its knowledge from different sciences; in the diagram below we can see two areas of knowledge connected to the object, or *what* to teach (language, culture), and two which are connected to the subjects, the *who* and the *how* of language teaching and learning.

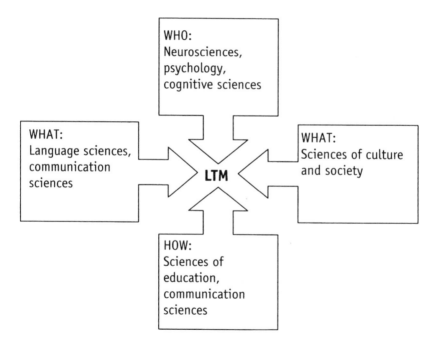

LTM is by necessity interdisciplinary, and brings the four areas together in a body of knowledge which is *not merely the sum of notions coming from different research areas but which constitute a new and independent branch of knowledge.*

5.1 Language and communication sciences

To give substance to the communicative approach which has dominated the language teaching scene for forty years, LTM has to look for areas of knowledge relating to four areas, as shown in the diagram above.

5.1.1 The nature of communication, of communicative events, and of communicative competence.

The communication sciences, from semiotics to ethnomethodology and ethnography of communication, are essential if we are to move beyond the superficial vision of the adjective 'communicative' which has characterised LTM for two generations.

The declared aim of language teaching is to develop 'communicative competence'. We shall devote an entire 'document' in this series to a description of the proposal made by the Venice group[8], but here we shall limit ourselves to noting that communicative competence is, to make use of a metaphor, a pyramid with four sides:

a. on the first side are the language skills, which make communication possible; only *cognitive sciences* can inform us about the processes which underlie speaking, reading, translating, summarizing, etc.;
b. the second side of the pyramid contains the functional dimension, or communicative acts: *sociolinguistics, pragmalinguistics, ethnolinguisticcs* and *intercultural communication studies* are the fundamental sciences required to shed light on this component of communicative competence;
c. on the third side we find verbal grammars, studied by *linguistics*, to which we shall return later;
d. finally, we find the non-verbal grammars: syllabus designers, materials writers, and teachers alike have to take into consideration kinesics, proxemics, and the use of clothes and objects for communicative purposes.

---

8 In a series published by Utet which contains contributions from the Venice school there is a volume on the relationship between communication sciences and LTM written by two researchers from the University of Florence, epistemologically close to the Venice school.

The LTM theoretician also needs to be acquainted with Chomskyan linguistics and the work of cognitive psychologists, which concern the nature of *competence* - a notion which cannot be treated approximately.

5.1.2 The notion of language and grammar

The first thing we need to consider when looking for a common basis underlying the complexity of LTM concerns universal grammar. Whether we are talking about first or second language, foreign or ethnic language, etc., we are always concerned with the *faculty of language*, common to all members of humankind, and the *universal grammar* which each person has, irrespective of the *linguistic typology* of their immediate language environment.

A second general problem concerns the differences between *descriptive, normative* and *pedagogic* grammars.

Although no longer in vogue, *comparative linguistics* also seems to have a fundamental part to play in the teaching and acquisition of languages other than the mother tongue: without wishing to make predictions about difficulty or grey areas, it is undeniable that many aspects of a learner's interlanguage can be explained (and modified) easily through reflecting from a comparative viewpoint.

5.1.3 Language as social act

We teach a language system (*langue*), we try to create competence in that system, but in LTM we do this with a precise aim: to produce *parole*, to ensure performance in a precise situational context. It is thus essential for LTM to consider the relationship between language and society both from a pragmatic-linguistic viewpoint, and from a sociolinguistic one[9].

5.1.4 Acquisitional linguistics

For the LTM methodologist this is another fundamental component of the language sciences.

Some commentators tend to equate this branch of linguistics with LTM,

---

9 In the series referred to in the previous note a researcher from the University of Bari, who studied with the Venice school, deals with the relationship between sociolinguistics and LTM (Santipolo 2002); on this subject see also Freddi (1999).

ignoring the fact that the first is concerned with acquisition and the second with acquisition *and* teaching.

Acquisitional linguistics has provided us, among other things, with a fundamental notion (the concept of *interlanguage*) and examines the natural order for the acquisition of grammar and lexis in any given language.

5.1.5 Non-verbal grammars

Lastly, we should not forget the study of semiotics and the logical structures of non-verbal languages which continually interplay with verbal languages.

If the aim of LTM is to perfect the *ability to communicate*, then research should not be limited just to verbal communication, but it should take into account kinesics, proxemics, vestemics and the use of objects for communicative purposes.

In the 21st century LTM has become complex because it cannot ignore any of these dimensions.

To give an example, and to clarify the type of complexity that this initial reflection requires, let us consider just one of the language sciences we have listed above, pragmalinguistics.

Pragmalinguistics offers a series of functional models: which of them can be productive in LTM? A simple analysis of the models devised by Cassirer, Bühler, Jakobson and Halliday, the four cornerstones of 20th century functional linguistics, will reveal that none of them are *applicable* to LTM: the methodologist must grasp any useful implications and come up with an integrated model which will resolve his problem of syllabus design (the central problem faced by the Council of Europe when attempting to establish all the *Threshold Levels*); once the macrofunctions are identified, the next step is to identify the communicative acts which comprise it (for example, the interpersonal function comprises communicative acts such as 'greeting', 'leave-taking', 'apologizing', etc.); for each of these acts a list of corresponding expressions needs to be drawn up ('exponents' in the functional-notional method), and to be classified on the basis of register, geographical variety, etc, and graded on the basis of frequency, order of acquisition and so on.

5.2 Sciences of culture and society

'When you teach a language, you also teach a culture' is the principle to which Giovanni Freddi devoted a lifetime of study and publications, from the beginning of the 1960's, when he founded the journal *Lingue e Civiltà* which has had a fundamental influence on the training of Italian teachers of foreign languages over the past twenty years.

'When you teach a language, you also teach a culture' is a maxim one hears everywhere, but in practice it often amounts to no more than offering a few stereotypes and the major cultural models of daily life. Two areas of study are fundamental here: (a) the definition of culture – both everyday culture and the culture with which we identify a specific group, and the set of beliefs and traditions which belong to it, which we shall call *civilisation* – and the type of interaction that exists between cultures; (b) the nature and problems of intercultural communication.

5.2.1 Culture, civilization, multi and inter-cultural society

Anthropology has given LTM two powerful concepts, namely the differences between *sterotype and sociotype*, and between *culture* and *clvilisation* (see 5.2 above).

It is one thing to teach cultural models, such as what people have for breakfast in Mediterranean countries or in the north of Europe, how to order things from the waiter, etc., and quite another thing to open the mind to the concept of food in different cultures, or to the concept of the relationship between customer and service provider.

If LTM wishes to provide instruments which will function in complex societies, it must first decide whether it wants to work towards the formation of *multicultural* societies (dominated by relativism and in which a language is only a means of making contact) or of *intercultural* societies (in which language is a means of contamination between cultural models, values, ways of viewing the world, and knowledge) [10].

---

10 This theme was fundamental in the Venice group's approach to teaching immigrants (Luise 2003); a 'document' in this series will be devoted to it. On culture and civilisation in foreign language teaching see Pavan 2006.

5.2.2 Problems of intercultural communication

This is a particularly complex sector, which has its own very recent specialist literature, and which is undergoing a process of continual epistemologic redefinition - but it is a fundamental sector for LTM in the 21st century; a Chinese person and a Brazilian who communicate using English as a lingua franca are still wholly Chinese and Brazilian in their values and in the way in which they conceive each other. Frequently it is intercultural miscomprehension, not a wrong use of a verb tense, which leads to a breakdown in communication[11].

a.2 Neurosciences, and psychological sciences, cognitive sciences

It is not enough to know a language and a culture to be able to teach them; knowledge of how the student's brain and mind work are equally important, and so the LTM methodologist has to turn to these sciences, too, to derive further implications.

5.3.1 Neurosciences and neurolinguistics

Acquisition cannot be made to happen without some understanding of how the brain works, i.e. of the brain's *hardware*.

This is an area of research in rapid expansion; only ten years ago Schumann's two most recent publications - *The Biological Foundations of Affect* and *The Biological Foundations of Language* would have attracted derision. Today neurological research, and in particular neurolinguistics, advances with every new issue of the specialist journals, due to non-invasive scanning techniques such as PET and MRI.

For example, to define the language policies of an education system, and to support early years language teaching, it is essential to know that up to the age of three non-lexical words are stored in the cerebellum as automatisms, while as the child grows older these words (pronouns, articles, prepositions, etc.) end up in the cortex, alongside lexical words, and are thus more difficult to use; but teachers need to have a good

---

11 The second 'document' in this series describes the Venice school's approach to the problem of intercultural communication, already outlined in Balboni 1999.

grasp of how this works, so as not to end up with an oversimplified model.

5.3.2 Psycholinguistics

The brain, then, is the hardware. We now have to turn to the system software, in other words the processes of the mind engaged in language acquisition, the *Language Acquisition Device*, or the mechanisms by which lexis is stored and recovered in the mental.

These are essential notions for the methodologist and they come from psycholinguistic research[12].

5.3.3 Cognitive psychology

This sector, which is now often seen as an autonomous group of sciences within the great family of cognitive sciences, gives LTM a number of fixed notions (such as the theories of *schemata*, *scripts* and *frames*) as well as variable elements such as types of intelligence, cognitive styles, and learning strategies which vary from one person to another and which lead to different attitudes and behaviour towards language learning in each individual.

5.3.4 Relational psychology

Teaching takes place in an environment of relations between learners, and between learners (as a group and as individuals) and the teacher. Unlike language classes in the Golden Age, which were homogenous and from which students with learning difficulties were excluded, complexity has now arrived in the classroom and mixed ability classes are the norm. Differentiation (which can derive from personal attitudes, types of intelligence, socio-cultural background, different types of motivation, etc.) makes the network of relations in the class extremely complex, to which the growing phenomenon of on-line teaching has

---

12 The neuro-psycholinguistic dimension is present in almost all work published by the Venice school; see in particular Freddi 1990 and 1999, and some of the works he commissioned in the 1980's - when such a choice seemed futuristic - for a series he edited, for example Danesi 1988 and Titone 1993; a young researcher from this school, Mario Cardona, now at the University of Bari, has recently continued work in this field (2001).

added a further dimension. This sector, too, is thus a significant area of research for LTM.

Secondly, relational problems are directly reflected in acquisition in that they may create an 'affective filter'.

Research into co-operative learning, into socially-orientated and constructivist methodologies are all relevant here.

5.3.5 Motivational psychology

The principle 'no acquisition without motivation' is well known; what is it, then, that motivates a language learner?

Renzo Titone, who taught in Venice at the beginning of the seventies, is the author of one of the best known motivational models, the holodynamic model, which provides a useful description of motivation for language acquisition as the interaction between the plans which the *ego* has for itself, the *strategies* which it devises to implement them, and the *tactical* phase in which the validity and efficiency of the strategies are put to the test. It is only through the balanced interaction of the here and now of the tactics and the long-term aims of the ego that a stable and lasting motivation can be created.

In our 1994 publication we developed another model - not an alternative to Titone's, but an integration of it. In the wake of sciences which study mass communications and advertising we identified three types of motivation:

- *duty*, which is useless for purposes of acquisition, with all the consequences which this simple statement can have on teaching;
- *need*, which may work for English as a lingua franca, or for immigrants seeking to integrate into a community, but which does not work for the study of languages other than English, or for ethnic or classical languages;
- and finally *pleasure*, the only constant source of motivation (a document in this series will be devoted to pleasure in language learning).

5.3.6 Psychology of identity

In some LTM contexts, such as bilingual education and the teaching of young immigrants (up to adolescence), it is also important to consider identity psychology and themes related to the development of the bilingual personality.

Just as there have been approaches based on the application of linguistics (or of a branch of lingustics, such as morpho-syntax in the grammar-translation approach), so too there are schools which *apply* pyschological theories but which completely ignore linguistic and anthropological research. These schools may be very interesting in themselves, but on the whole they are unable to generate innovation; examples of these are *Suggestopedia*, developed by Lozanov, and Curran's *Counselling Learning*.

5.4 Education sciences

A teacher - whether of languages, history, or mathematics - needs to have a background in

a. *principles of education*
b. *teaching methodology*
c. *teaching technologies*
d. *testing and evaluation*

and should also be able to adapt this knowledge to the specific teaching context - whether teaching children or adults, in a school or for a company, in an educational environment or simply in a context of instruction or training. There is no need for us here to take space to describe these areas of knowledge, which we take for granted.

Nonetheless, it is worth noting that language teaching has a feature which is not shared by any other subject-related teaching (such as the teaching of mathematics or art): the *end* and the *means* by which it is achieved are one and the same. *A language is taught by using the language*. If this is not a problem for the mother tongue, it becomes problematic with the choice of the language of instruction for second, foreign and ethnic languages; the complexity of the problem varies from one moment to another, and from case to case.

5.5 Synthesis

If we add the epistemological reflections of the previous chapters to this interdisciplinary model of LTM, we realize that a LTM based on *application* is no longer possible, since there are too many sciences involved, and each has its own research methods and its own language for processing knowledge.

This interdisplinary nature implies a double risk: on the one hand, of providing a justification for the dilettante, on the other hand of overwhelming the serious researcher who is well aware that he will never be able to master all the disciplines involved.

And here we come to the great challenge of LTM: to avoid becoming a patchwork quilt (or a Harlequin's coat, to use Freddi's metaphor) by stitching together bits of different cloth in a haphazard manner. This is too big a challenge for one person, both profound and far-reaching. The epistemological complexity of LTM requires complex research structures; not just a handful of individuals, but work groups and networks of researchers, which can transcend individual departments, PhD programmes and universities and which are increasingly open to interaction with the scientific community at large, and by working closely with it, to rise to the challenge.

6. From a simple to a complex perspective: a historical sketch

We have based this first 'document' on the assumption that LTM has moved from a simple model to one which has become gradually more complex.

To illustrate this, here is a simplified timeline. Of course many methods and approaches which are in decline have not disappeared completely, even if we remove them from the table at a particular date:

Approaches and methods	Period
Grammar-translation approach	Dominant at the beginning of the 20th century
Direct approach (known as 'method'), Berlitz approach	Beginning of the 20th century
Reading approach (known as 'method')	Between the two World Wars
Army Specialised Training Program (ASTP)	Second World War
Audio-lingual approach, structuralist approach	1950's- 1960's
Comunicative approach: - situational method - clinical methods (suggestopaedia, counselling learning, etc.) - notional-functional method (known as 'approach'); affective-humanistic connotations, NLP, ICT use, certification logic have been added from the 1990s	1960's-1970's 1970's-1980's 1970's-1990's 1990's to present

As has been noted, some approaches have gone down in history as 'methods', even though they were full-blown philosophies of language and language teaching; whereas the communicate approach incorporates a variety of methods which have given expression to it, with each new method generally retaining most of the principles of the previous methods. The basic expression of the communicative approach, which is the notional-functional method 'topped up' with elements from previous approaches, has had the support in recent years of specific methodologies and, thanks to the European Portfolio which derives from the Common European Framework, is directly linked to the official certifiable levels of proficiency established by the Council of Europe. To chart the progress of LTM over the past century we shall now briefly examine some of the aspects associated with different approaches.

6.1 The linguistic dimension

Two interesting features of the linguistic dimension are the shifting emphasis between analysis and use of language, and the debate about *langue* and *parole*.

6.1.1 Analysis and use

The emphasis on *analysis* or *use* of language, and consequently on the phases of skill getting (*usage*, to use Widdowson's term) or skill using (*use,* for Widdowson) has led to many historians of LTM to refer to a 'pendulum syndrome' because of a noticeable oscillation between the two.

The nineteenth century focussed on analysis and grammar, which led to a reaction by scholars (Jespersen, Palmer, Sweet) and an elite clientele who could afford a mother tongue teacher using the direct method proposed by Berlitz in 1896, based on using the language.

American isolationism and European dictatorships between the wars, which prevented the movement of people between countries, pushed the pendulum towards reading skills, since if people couldn't be moved, at least books and essays could; then, as World War II approached, the urgency of the situation led to a new focus on use, which became the situational approach of ASTP, with a strong interest in the cultural dimension, known as *area studies*.

The period dominated by Bloomfield, Skinner and Lado moved the pendululm back towards analysis and the dissection of language into tiny components, but from Fishman and Hymes on the emphasis has been firmly on use and communication.

6.1.2 Language as 'langue' and 'parole'

At the beginning of the 20th century the emphasis was on *langue*, the language viewed as a system; this was followed, a long time before the official beginning of sociolinguistics, by a move towards *parole*, the language which is actually produced in a specific context.

This clearly happened in response to a recognition of the social dimension of language, but it entailed moving from the internal complexity of the system (the language with all its internal articulations and mechanisms) to an external complexity (the language has to adapt to the context - a context which has become dramatically changeable in recent decades).

6.2 The anthropological and sociological dimension

The ASTP of the American military was a watershed: the ideas of Berlitz had a socio-anthropological dimension, and there were reflections on the relationship between language and culture in the work done by Malinowsky, but it was with the war and the ASTP that the need to teach everyday culture became apparent; the structuralist approach brought an a-cultural parenthesis (even if one of the major exponents, Robert Lado, was the author of *Linguistics across Cultures*) but from the sixties culture was once again seen as a fundamental element of communication and consequently of the communicative approach.

In recent years the problems of intercultural communication, due both to the use of English as a lingua franca in the global economy and to the great migratory movements of people, has become central to the theoretical debate, even if still absent in everyday practice; this dimension will dominate the future of LTM.

6.3 The neurological and psychological dimension

There has been continual progress on a number of levels:

a. attention to *the way the brain functions*: until the 1950's little was
   known on the subject, and in any case the focus of the formalistic
   and immediately operative approaches of the Direct method and the
   Reading method was far removed from the idea that the brain might
   be a variable to be taken into consideration. In recent decades an
   interest in the neurosciences has grown steadily, and is modifying
   the way we think about language teaching and as a consequence,
   the courses, materials and teaching procedures we adopt.;
b. attention to *aquisition mechanisms*: progress has been similar to
   that in the neurosciences, and has led to the incorporation of NLP
   and acquisitional linguistics into LTM, and an emphasis on the
   humanistic/affective dimension and Goleman's emotional intelligence;
c. attention to *motivation*: the communicative approach places
   motivation firmly at the centre of the teaching/learning process. In
   the grammar translation approach motivation is irrelevant, since the
   student *must* study the classical or foreign language for social reasons,
   independently of any real interest he has for the language; with
   ASTP motivation changes and becomes ideological - to learn the
   language becomes important to win the war, and later, the cold war;
   the structuralist approach focuses on the language and its structure,
   ignoring the motivational component, but from the 1960's the role
   of motivation based on needs appears: to know languages is necessary
   to be able to interact in a globalizing economy. The European policy
   of promoting languages other than English, together with the need
   to keep the teaching of 'useless' languages - French, German, Italian
   and Spanish - and the desire of many people to belong to specific
   groups (see chapter 1) means that the main source of motivation to
   (continue to) learn languages is based on pleasure;
d. the *relational dimension* too has seen a similar development; until
   the 1960's each student was an isolated individual; but over the last
   thirty years the relations between students in the class have steadily
   gained importance, while the teacher-student relation, which had
   been unidirectional in the approaches favoured in the first half of

the century, became more and more interactive. The role of the teacher was simple: she had to know the language and decide what was right or wrong; today, the teacher produces output, is a reference point in case of doubt, is a group leader, a tutor for individual students, an on-line seeker of resources and also the one who corrects errors.

It is clear that in this dimension, linked to the neurosciences and to psychological aspects, both the volume of research and social pressures have created an extremely complex backdrop where once, with a formalistic approach, it was very simple: the teacher knows the language, the student doesn't, the teacher transmits his or her knowledge to the student, who has to learn what the teacher believes to be correct, or fail. Today such a model is inconceivable.

6.4 The educational and methodological dimension

Over the years the relations between the three components of the teaching act - language, student, and teacher - have changed profoundly.

a. the *language* was at the centre of this relational network in the approaches favoured until the 1960's; teaching programmes were based on requirements of the language system (such as completion and correctness); in the decades which followed the attention shifted to the needs and interests of the student. Until the 1950's the language was complete and perfect, it was viewed as *langue*, with its rules and its exceptions. With Fishman the concept of language is transformed radically - it is no longer a changeless and perfect *langue* but a system made up of numerous varieties, geographical and specialist, which integrate with non verbal languages, with multimedia contexts, and so on;
b. the *student* in the structuralist or grammar based approaches was an empty container which had to be filled with notions about the language. Only with the communicative approach did the student become an important factor in the teaching process, and, in the last decades of the century, the central, crucial element;
c. during the first half of the century the *teacher* was the high priest of

Paolo E. Balboni

the book of grammar, the model of the language and the judge who never failed; as the years passed, this role changed, albeit more in theory than in practice. The teacher became what Bruner calls the *Language Acquisition Support System* capable of activating the *Language Acquisition Device* hypothesised by Chomsky, a complex 'system' of roles and functions, and no longer the simple oracle of grammar.

6.5 Synthesis

The progression, as we have seen, has been coherent; from the centrality of the language as structure, which a confident teacher transmits to an ignorant student, there has been a slow movement towards an environment in which

a. the word 'language' is replaced by the concept 'communicate with language';
b. the neuro-psychological and relational complexity of the learner has been recognized;
c. the teacher has become the director of operations, who, as Humboldt put it, creates the conditions for acquisition to take place.

The progression from a simple to a complex background to language teaching has been truly dramatic; and educational systems, materials writers and publishers, institutions which plan teacher training are all moving, slowly but steadily, in the direction of acknowledging and dominating this complexity which LTM (not just the Venice school, of course) has been systematically describing for decades.

References

This 'Document' is intended for experts, and so it is not necessary here to refer to the works of Chomsky, Bruner, Lado, Krashen, Byram or the Council of Europe, which are all widely known. This bibliography contains only those works emerging from, or published in collaboration with, the Venice group - for the sole reason of making it possible, for whoever is interested, to find out more about the topics dealt with in the paper.

BALBONI P.E. 1991, *Tecniche didattiche per l'educazione linguistica [Techniques for Language Education]*, Torino, Petrini (new edition: 1998, Utet Libreria).

BALBONI P.E. 1994 *Didattica dell'italiano a stranieri [Teaching Italian as a Foreign Language]*, Roma, Bonacci.

BALBONI P. E. 1999, *Dizionario di glottodidattica [Dictionary of Language Teaching Methodology]*, Perugia, Guerra.

BALBONI P. E. 1999, *Parole comuni, culture diverse. Guida alla comprensione interculturale [Common Words, Different Cultures. A Guide to Intercultural Communication]*, Venezia, Marsilio.

BALBONI P.E, (ed.) 2000, *Approccio alla Lingua Italiana per Allievi Stranieri [An Approach to Teaching Italian as a Second Language]*, Torino, Theorema.

BALBONI P. E. 2002, *Le sfide di Babele. Insegnare le lingue nelle società complesse [The Challenge of Babel. Teaching Languages in Complex Societies]*, Torino, Utet Libreria.

BORELLO E., B. BALDI, 2003, *Scienze della comunicazione e glottodidattica [Sciences of Communication and Language Teaching Methodology]*, Torino, Utet Libreria.

CAON F., 2005, *Un approccio umanistico-affettivo all'insegnamento dell'italiano a non nativi, [An Affective-Humanistic Approach to the Teaching of Italian to Non-Native Speakers]*, Venezia, Cafoscarina, 2005.

Caon F., S. Rutka 2004, *La lingua in gioco [Playing with Language]*, Perugia, Guerra.

Caon F., B. D'Annunzio 2006, *Il laboratorio di Italiano L2 [Laboratories in Italian as a Seconda Language]*, Perugia, Guerra.

Cardona M. 2001, *Il ruolo della memoria nell'apprendimento delle lingue [The Role of Memory in Language Learning]*, Torino, Utet Libreria.

Celentin P., E. Cognigni 2005, *Insegnare l'italiano a studenti di origine slava [Teaching Italian to Slavonic Students]*, Perugia, Guerra.

Coonan C. M. 2001, *La lingua straniera veicolare [Content and Language Integrated Learning]*, Torino, Utet Libreria.

Danesi M. 1988, *Neurolinguistica e glottodidattica [Neurolinguistics and Language Teaching Methodology]*, Torino, Liviana-Petrini.

D'Annunzio 2006 (forthcoming), *Insegnare l'italiano a studenti di origine cinese [Teaching Italian to Chinese Students]*, Perugia, Guerra.

Della Puppa F., 2005, *Insegnare l'italiano a studenti di origine araba [Teaching Italian to Arab Students]*, Perugia, Guerra.

Dolci R., P. Celentin 2003, *La formazione di base del docente di italiano per stranieri [A Handbook for the Formation of the Teachers of Italian as a Foreign Language]*, Roma, Bonacci.

Freddi G. 1970, *Metodologia e didattica delle lingue straniere [Foreing Language Teaching Methodology]*, Bergamo, Minerva Italica.

Freddi G. 1979, *Didattica delle lingue moderne [Modern Language Teaching]*, Bergamo, Minerva Italica.

Freddi G. 1990, *Il bambino e la lingua. Psicolinguistica e glottodidattica [The Child and Language. Psycholinguistics and Language Teaching Methodology]*, Torino, Liviana-Petrini.

Freddi G. 1994, *Glottodidattica: fondamenti, metodi e tecniche [Language Teaching Methodology. Foundations, Methods, Techniques]*, Torino, Utet Libreria.

Freddi G. 1999, *Psicolinguistica, Sociolinguistica, Glottodidattica. La formazione di base dell'insegnante di lingue e di lettere [Psycholinguistics, Sociolinguistics, Language Teaching Methodology. The Basics of the Formation of the Teacher of Italian and Foreign Languages]*, Torino, Utet Libreria.

Luise M. C. (ed.) 2003, *Italiano lingua seconda. Fondamenti e metodi [Italian as a Second Language. Foundations and Methodology]*, Guerra, Perugia.

Luise M. C. 2006 (forthcoming), *Insegnare le lingue seconde [Teaching Second Languages]*, Torino, Utet Libreria.

PAVAN E. 2005, *Il 'lettore' di italiano. Formazione linguistica e glottodidattica [The Language Assistant of Italian Abroad. Linguistic and Methodological Formation]*, Roma, Bonacci.

PAVAN E. 2006 (forthcoming), *Cultura, civiltà e interculturalità nell'insegnamento delle lingue [Culture, Civilisation and Interculturality in Language Teaching]*, Torino, Utet Libreria.

PORCELLI G. e P. E. BALBONI (eds) 1991, *Glottodidattica e università. La formazione del Professore di Lingue [Language Teaching Methodology in Universities. The Formation of the Language Teacher]*, Torino, Liviana-Petrini.

PORCELLI G. e R. DOLCI 1999, *Multimedialità e insegnamenti linguistici [Multimedia and Language Teaching]*, Torino, Utet Libreria.

SANTIPOLO M. 2002, *Dalla sociolinguistica alla glottodidattica [From Sociolinguistics to Language Teaching Methodology]*, Torino, Utet Libreria.

SANTIPOLO M. 2005, *Italiano dentro e fuori d'Italia [Teaching Italian Inside and Outside Italy]*, Torino, Utet Libreria.

SERRAGIOTTO G. 2003, *Apprendere insieme una lingua e contenuti non linguistici [Content and Language Integrated Learning]*, Perugia, Guerra.

SERRAGIOTTO G. (ed.) 2004, *Le lingue straniere nella scuola. Nuovi percorsi, nuovi ambienti, nuovi docenti [Foreign Languages in Schools. New Curricula, New Environments, New Teachers]*, Utet Libreria, Torino.

TITONE R., 1973 "The Psycholinguistic Definition of the 'Glossodynamic Model' of Language Behavior and Language Learning', in *R.I.L.A.*, 3.

TITONE R. 1993, *Psicopedagogia e glottodidattica [Psychopedagogy and Language Teaching Methodology]*, Padova, Liviana.

Finito di stampare
nel mese di marzo 2006
da Guerra guru srl - Perugia
Tel. +39 075 5289090 - Fax +39 075 5288244
e-mai:geinfo@guerra-edizioni.com